New Author Trauma: When The Dream Is Snatched!

by

L.Y. Hendry

Copyright ©2024 by L. Y. Hendry

All Rights Reserved.

ISBN: 9798325710018
Imprint: Independently published

Introduction: A Dreamer's Ambition

My name is Latonia Yvette Wiggins-Hendry, a bright and tenacious woman whose heart beats with the rhythm of words and stories. With a well-worn notebook always at my side and a mind brimming with imagination, I was a hopeful and aspiring author, ready to conquer the literary world one word at a time.

Growing up in a small town, I found solace in the pages of books that transported me to far-off lands and introduced me to characters who felt like friends. As I navigated the many ups and downs of life, I discovered my own voice through writing; pouring my thoughts and dreams onto the pages of my notebook. My words became a refuge, a place where I could shape my reality and explore my creativity.

Despite the challenges that life often presented, my determination and passion for storytelling remained unwavering. I devoured books of all genres, gleaning insights into different narrative techniques and writing styles, all the while dreaming of my own name adorning the spines of bookshelves. As I grew older, I traded my old notebook for a computer and then a laptop. My days were filled with tapping away at my laptop, capturing the worlds and characters that inhabited my mind. Each keystroke brought me closer to my goal.

My journey was not without obstacles. Rejections from friends and family telling me I was wasting my time tested my resolve but they never extinguished my fervor. I attended many writing workshops and conferences seeking guidance from established authors and polishing my skills with the feedback of my peers. As I honed in on my craft, I also formed a close-knit circle of fellow aspiring writers who offered both camaraderie and constructive critique.

My pursuit of success was driven not just by a desire for recognition, but also by a genuine love for storytelling. I believed, and still do believe, in the power of words to connect, inspire, and transform. I wanted to write about characters that were extensions of myself; bearing fragments of my experiences, hopes, and fears. Through them, I explored themes of resilience, love, and the human spirit, inviting readers to reflect on their own lives.

I embodied the spirit of an eager dreamer which fueled my passion for literature and the promise of sharing my unique voice with the world. As I set forth on my journey to make my mark in the literary landscape, my unyielding determination and boundless creativity was interrupted by a memory from my past that took my life in another direction. After that life-changing experience, I no longer wanted to write about characters like me but wanted to write about the revelations of my life that were buried in my subconscious. I knew my story would shape not only my destiny but also the hearts of those who would be able to move from pain to purpose from reading my work. I knew that becoming a published author held a special allure that transcends time and cultures. It is a dream that has been pursued by countless individuals, fueled by a combination of personal ambition and the allure of literary success. The allure lies in the power of words to capture thoughts, emotions, and stories, and to share them with the world. I wanted that feeling that countless others have experienced. I wanted my passion to finally be able to transcend in book-form.

There is a unique sense of immortality in the act of creating something that can outlive the author, leaving a lasting impact on readers for generations to come. The very thought of having a body of work that my great great-grandchildren could read, and be proud of, gave me a sense of wanting to get the finished product done as soon as possible.

After doing some research, along with my own desire to see my work in print, I discovered that the dreams that fuel the ambition of aspiring authors are diverse and deeply personal. Here are some of the key factors that contribute to their allure:

Creative Expression: Writing offers an avenue for unbridled creative expression. The idea of crafting intricate worlds, developing complex characters, and weaving captivating plots is immensely appealing. Authors relish the opportunity to translate their thoughts and imagination onto the pages of a book, leaving a tangible mark of their inner world.

Legacy: The desire to leave a legacy is a powerful motivator. Authors know that their stories can carry on long their life is over and that gives them the ability to connect with readers and sparking emotions long after they are gone. The thought of contributing something meaningful to the literary canon is incredibly enticing.

Validation and Recognition: Many authors seek validation for their thoughts, ideas, and talents. Being published is often seen as an affirmation of their worth as writers; providing a sense of accomplishment and recognition for their efforts.

Impact: Authors dream of touching lives through their words. They aspire to inspire, provoke thought, and evoke emotions in readers. The notion that a book can change someone's perspective, offer solace, or ignite a passion is a driving force for many.

Financial Success: While not the primary motivation for all authors, the possibility of financial success cannot be overlooked. The idea of making a living doing what they love, and potentially achieving fame and fortune, is an appealing prospect.

Escape and Exploration: Writing allows authors to escape the confines of reality and explore new realms. This creative exploration can be both liberating and therapeutic, offering a way to cope with life's challenges and uncertainties.

My journey as a new author did not come easy. The excitement I felt after having experienced a life-long dream was literally snatched from under me. The hurt and shame I felt after going through such a horrible experience left me scared and anxious for a long time.

I have talked about my experience briefly to friends, family, on my podcast 'A Womans Soul: Restored', and after being asked countless times to write about my trauma from being a first-time author, I have decided to share the lessons I have learned along the way in hopes that another aspiring author would not have to suffer the pain that I did.

"My prayer is that this book blesses you and causes you to do your due diligence when something sounds too good to be true!"

Chapter 1: The Dream Becoming a Reality

For new authors, the journey from -thought to outline to manuscript to published book- is a mixture of vulnerability and excitement. The vulnerability comes from exposing their inner thoughts and feelings to the world, knowing that their work will be open to criticism and scrutiny. The fear of rejection, both from publishers and readers, can be daunting. This vulnerability can be compounded by the personal nature of their writing; which often reflects their own experiences, beliefs, and emotions.

However, amidst this vulnerability, there is also an undeniable excitement. The prospect of sharing their stories with a wider audience, and of finally seeing their words in print, is a thrilling adventure. Every aspiring author yearns for that pivotal moment when their book is accepted by a publisher, or when they self-publish, and see their work available to the public. It is a journey filled with hope, anticipation, and a sense of accomplishment.

Wide-eyed and ready for a publisher to pick up my book was something I had always dreamed about. After being in an abusive relationship, where my ex-husband told me that I was wasting **his** –not a typo- time with writing and to stop, the idea of actually having written a book and moving to the next phase was too much excitement to contain. I had seen advertisers on television with information about publishing so I had submitted my work to a few publishers. I really wanted this venture to be a success and to be able to leave my mark on history; plus a little money would not hurt either.

Now let's dive into a cool moment! I was going about my day here in beautiful Savannah, Georgia. I had poured my heart and soul into my writing and was dreaming of sharing my insights and stories with the world. One sunny afternoon, while sipping on a banana and strawberry smoothie and checking emails on my laptop at a local restaurant in the bustling downtown area, I received an email that caught my full attention. It was from a well-known publishing company expressing interest in my work. My heart raced as I read through the message with excitement building with each line. This unexpected opportunity felt like a door swinging open to a new chapter in my journey. With a mix of joy and expectation, I knew that my hard work and dedication were finally catching the right eyes. It was a moment that would fuel my passion even further and set me on a path towards achieving my goal of writing more books and ultimately reaching a wider audience.

When a new author submits their manuscript, it is a mix of excitement and nervousness. I had poured my heart and soul into my book-my true story, spent countless hours writing, and now I was at the point where someone important was saying I was ready to share my creation with the world.

I can still remember that feeling, like it was yesterday, of accomplishment and joy when I received that email within a week of me sending out my manuscript. This very act affirmed that they loved my story and could see it being a number one seller. My heart was beaming as I was telling everyone I knew about what was about to happen. I was sending out group texts, and calling those that I knew did not like group text messages, to tell them about my news. The dream was about to become a reality and I was beside myself. A Published Author...ME? The way my life had progressed through the years, I figured it was time that I experienced some happiness and success like I had witnessed countless of others achieving. I had so much to do, and I was ready to do whatever they asked. They requested more information from me and even asked me to have a lawyer look over my contract. When I did everything they asked me-I will get into that later, and my contract was signed, I was well on the way to becoming the next big name in the literary world. I could not be happier.

The allure of becoming a published author is a complex blend of creative passion, personal ambition, and the dream of leaving a lasting impact. The vulnerability of new authors is juxtaposed with the excitement of sharing their work and creating a journey that is both challenging and rewarding. The world of writing and publishing is a realm where vulnerability and excitement coexist, fostering a unique camaraderie among authors who share these dreams.

New authors often feel susceptible because they are putting their creative work out into the world not knowing how it will be received. They might have spent months or even years pouring their heart and soul into their writing, and the prospect of rejection or criticism can be overwhelming. It is like opening a piece of your inner world for everyone to explore and review. In 2015, as a new author, I could relate to the vulnerabilities that new authors experience when seeking opportunities in the world of publishing.

On the flip side, there is a level of explosiveness that cannot be denied. The idea of seeing your name in print, sharing your stories or ideas with a wider audience and connecting with readers who resonate with your work can be incredibly thrilling. Embarking on a new adventure full of possibilities would be enticing to anyone going into any type of new venture.

For new authors, it is important to persevere through the trials and savor the excitement. It is also wise to explore various publishing opportunities, from traditional publishing houses to self-publishing, to find the path that suits their goals and aspirations best. Writing communities, workshops, and networking can also be invaluable on this journey. So, while it may be a rollercoaster ride, it is a journey filled with potential and growth. The excitement comes from the anticipation of seeing your work in print and sharing your ideas and stories with readers. The mere thought of people actually reading your work is a RUSH of adrenaline. You might be envisioning your book on shelves or getting positive reviews from readers who connect with your words-Book reviews are critical to a books success. It is like a dream slowly coming true. There is also trepidation. You are sending your work out into the world, and that can be nerve-wracking. You wonder if it is good enough, if people will like it, or if it will even get accepted by a publisher. There is a fear of rejection, which is a common feeling among authors.

There is also a fear that your work may get stolen. You really have to have a level of trust when you are submitting your work to others that you do not even know personally and extending their trustworthiness through reading reviews and reputable websites. Each submission is a leap of faith but it is all part of the journey toward becoming a successful author and achieving your goals. Keep pushing forward, and your passion for writing and storytelling will guide you through both the excitement and the apprehension but you have to be very careful.

Let us take a sidebar as I introduce you to a common character in the world of publishing: the charismatic agent or publisher who preys on a new authors' dreams. This person often presents themselves as a well-connected and experienced professional in the publishing industry. They may promise new authors fame, fortune, and literary success. They will use their charisma and persuasive skills to gain the trust of aspiring writers. They have to master this skill in order to be successful at what they do; which is finding victims!

Here are some warning signs to watch out for when dealing with such individuals:

Upfront Fees: They might ask for substantial upfront fees for various services like editing, marketing, or publishing.

Legitimate agents and publishers typically earn a commission from book sales rather than charging authors upfront. This is not an immediate red flag, but is an indicator that you should keep your eyes and ears open and your senses keen!

Vague Promises: Be cautious if their promises seem too good to be true. Success in the publishing world is often the result of hard work, talent, and persistence, not instant fame and riches. They use words to make you feel special and to weaken you by making you feel at ease and that everything they are telling you is the honest truth.

Lack of Transparency: A trustworthy agent or publisher will be transparent about their fees, processes, and the likelihood of success. If they are evasive, or unwilling to provide clear information, it is a red flag. Contracts are explicit, direct, and legally binding. Anything beyond what is written is something you should not pay attention or buy into.

Pressure to Sign Quickly: Scammers may pressure you to make quick decisions by claiming that opportunities are limited. Take your time to research and consider any offer thoroughly. The "Hurry or Rush" technique is one to get you to <u>act</u> rather than <u>think</u>. Spontaneous decisions are often wrong decisions.

Unprofessional Behavior: Watch out for unprofessional behavior, such as poor communication, missed deadlines, or failure to deliver on promises. Also be care of a representative being overly friendly. They try to make you feel comfortable as quickly as possible so the scam can be accomplished as soon as possible.

Check Credentials: Research the agent or publisher's background, client reviews, and track record. Legitimate professionals have a history of successful author relationships. There may be some bad, but it should be extensively more good than bad.

Trust Your Instincts: This is one that is often overlooked and underrated but vitally important. If something does not feel right, trust your instincts. It is better to walk away from a questionable deal than to get caught up in a scam.

To protect your writing dreams, it is essential to be cautious and do your due diligence when dealing with agents or publishers. Seek recommendations, verify credentials, and be prepared to ask tough questions. A new author may feel like they are hurting the publishers' feelings, or undermining their reputation by being too thorough, but you have to put measures in place to protect yourself. Their feelings are not going to be hurt if they have nothing to hide and they are really looking out for your best interest. Remember that success in the writing world often comes from talent, hard work, and finding the right partners who genuinely support your career and are honest.

Chapter 2: The Web of Illusion

Scammers can be quite manipulative, especially in the publishing industry. Here is a simplified overview of how my situation unfolded:

Initial Contact: The scammer that reached out to me was a real publishing agent, who praised my work and expressed interest in my writing. They were one of the companies I reached out to with my manuscript. For the sake of this book, and so I will not get sued, we will call them Bait Publishing.

Flattery and Promises: To gain my trust, Bait Publishing continued to flatter me throughout the scam, saying they see great potential in my work. They promised to help me become a successful author, making me feel special and valued.

Request for Money: Gradually, they introduce various fees for services like editing, cover design, and marketing. They claimed these expenses were necessary for my book's success. This is where the manipulation started. They pressured me into paying these fees and made it seem like it was for the benefit of my success. They were so smooth about it until it did not feel like pressure at all.

False Guarantees: Bait assured me that once I paid the fees, my book would be a bestseller, and I would make a lot of money. They showed me reviews that turned out to be fake success stories.

*No one can guarantee anything at a 100% level. Let this be a definite red flag of deceptive practices.

Isolation: Initially, Bait suggested that I get outside advice from a lawyer but then they discouraged me from seeking advice from others. They made me believe that their plan was the only way to succeed. This isolated me from potential sources of help and advice.

*At the time, my oldest sister worked at a law firm and knew a lot about contracts. I took it to her, and she suggested that I question them on some things, but I got caught up in the hype and I did not do my due diligence.

Additional Demands: As I continued to cooperate and invest money-and we are not talking about a little amount, Bait came up with more reasons to ask for additional funds, always promising that success is just around the corner.

Unfulfilled Promises: I did see initial success with the book climbing to a popular website best seller- more about that later. Despite my total investments and seeing some success, my book did not achieve the success promised; not even a fraction of it. Eventually they became evasive when I finally began to ask questions.

"In other words, they sold me some horse manure and I brought all of it and some in reserves!"

This book is a full disclosure of what happened to me to help you avoid falling victim to such scams as I did. ALWAYS research publishing agents thoroughly, seek recommendations from trusted sources, and never pay large sums up front. Legitimate publishing professionals typically earn money through royalties, not upfront fees.

If you suspect you have encountered a scam, it is crucial to cease contact with the individual or entity, report them to relevant authorities or platforms, and seek legal advice, if necessary, as soon as possible. Your writing talents are valuable and there are genuine professionals who can help you without resorting to those that will use manipulation or scams.

Here are a few specific tactics Bait used to make me feel valued and special:

Personal Attention: I received individual attention from higher ups in the company. This was supposed to show that I was important to them and my work mattered.

Recognition: They sent me a list of the achievements I would be recognized for. I was praised by the team that was supposed to be my support system. They did all of this to make me feel valued and to drop my guard.

Supportive Relationships: I formed a special bond with my assigned agent. She was always checking on me and questioning me about ordering more books and setting up book tours. It all seemed like it was in my best interest to go full speed ahead.

Challenges and Growth: They set up workshops for me that was supposed to connect me with industry leaders and get my book before producers for a possible TV show or movie.

*I found out, after the fact, that this is a dead giveaway for a scam. The allure of a possible movie or TV show pulls aspiring authors in and makes them spend more money.

Unique Abilities: I was made to feel like I had special skills and qualities within my writing that set me apart and honestly it made me feel exceptional.

Symbolic Gifts or Gestures: They lured me in fully by doing one thing in particular that made me believe and buy more of what they were selling-more about that to come.

Empowerment: Bait allowed me to seem like I was making important decisions and they filled me with fancies of a best seller and a better life for my family.

Remember, a scammer will do or say anything to make that connection between you and them to get all the money they can get out of you as fast as they can. They must be really engaging and pull you into their writing web of deceit.

They master these tactics to make you feel comfortable and to value what they are selling!

They did their best to keep me more invested in the relationship emotionally and financially. It is like watching a flower bloom and bad weather comes and strong winds rip away all the beautiful petals. It takes methodical steps for this to happen. At first, they might make it seem like they are curious about what is going on in your personal life. They start spending more time asking less business questions and they begin sharing stories and experiences about themselves as well. They use this bonding technique to learn more about you. You think they are talking to you about themselves but they are pulling information out of you through general conversations. This is what makes it succeed most of the time.

Small gestures and acts of kindness come naturally to the scammer and always move on a victim emotionally. It causes them to believe the scammer, spend more money, and ask less questions. I found myself thinking about was I doing the right thing, but that was the purpose of Bait keeping in touch with me; to keep me from thinking and trusting them more. The more I opened up about my thoughts and feelings about regular issues and concerns, the deeper the connection became. It was almost like we were facing challenges and obstacles together and this made the bond even stronger. In some instances, I would be the one to call. It seemed like I had a new best friend.

The emotional investment is what is needed to deepen the relationship. Money is something that can be replaced, but when you have been hurt by people you trusted, this takes longer to recover from. It is like a gardener tending to a garden with care, but over time, he destroys the thing he once beautified.

Think of it like a journey:

Ever since I can remember, I had wanted to be a writer. I used to write poetry in elementary school. I was considered a nerd, with my thick glasses and worn notebook, but I did not care. I had my love of words and it took me on a voyage far away from real life. I could go wherever I wanted to and do anything. Words were my escape from many things in life and that did not change as I became an adult. A journey of a made-up reality that was a comfort from my actual reality and the horrors that came with it. The pencil and paper were a lovely escape to anywhere.

A deep investment:

I opened up about my thoughts and feelings. I shared many personal 'isms with my agent. This vulnerability brought us closer over the phone. She made every effort to be supportive and understanding; acting like she genuinely cared. Personally, I do not have the heart to do anyone like what was done to me but you must have a special kind of persona to carry out a diabolical scheme to get money from someone by any means necessary.

In the end, the emotional investment is one where you reach a point that you cannot imagine how this could happen to you.

How could you mistake the bond?

How strong could you really be if you were so easily fooled?

How can you face your family and friends and tell them you were conned?

Will you ever see the money again that was stolen?

How can you ever trust yourself, or anyone else, ever again?

The journey of going from dream to scam will take an emotional toll on you that you never felt in your life. This is a true test of survival.

Chapter 3: The Mirage of Investment

Scammers often try to trick people by posing as marketing or editing service providers. They might promise big returns on investments (ROI) if you give them money upfront for their services. They play on your desire for success and offer too-good-to-be-true deals. They might sound persuasive, but it is vitally important to be cautious. Legitimate businesses do not usually ask for money upfront. If you are ever unsure, it is great to research the company, check reviews, and talk to someone you trust before making any financial decisions.

It is unfortunate that scammers sometimes try to take advantage of people's trust but that is what makes them good at what they do. They have to reel you in like a fish on a hook. They will probe to see what areas you need the most help without you realizing that is what they are doing. In these situations, they might reach out pretending to offer marketing, editing, or other services after discovering that is your need. They will make it sound like a great opportunity to invest money, promising big returns. However, their main goal is to get your money and disappear without providing any real service. Always be cautious and double-check the legitimacy of any such offers before making any financial commitments. If something sounds too good to be true, it is always great to follow your gut. Our natural instincts alert us but we push it to the back of our minds and proceed forward with what we want to do. Do not dismiss how you feel before proceeding forward. Take your feelings into consideration.

Imagine being caught up in making a big decision. You may be torn between using your money for something else important and taking a risk to invest. Inside your head, thoughts are like a ping-pong game. On one side, you really want the potential rewards of investing and like achieving a financial status that would allow to not having to wait on payday anymore or being able to help others. But on the other side, you are worried about what if things go wrong and you lose the money that you cannot really afford to lose. It is like you are standing at a crossroads, trying to balance your dreams and the reality of your financial situation. After a lot of back-and-forth, you take a deep breath and go for it. You decide to invest, understanding the risks but also believing in the possibilities. It is a tough call, but your hope for a better future wins over your fear of failure. Maybe you have lived a life of being reserved and figured that this time, this change will be the best decision you will ever make.

It is disastrous how scammers often target people's emotions and vulnerabilities. They can exploit feelings of trust, fear, and even desperation to manipulate individuals into giving up their money or personal information. It is essential to stay cautious and skeptical when encountering suspicious requests, especially online or through unsolicited communications. Being aware of these tactics can help protect yourself and others from falling victim to scams. If you have any concerns about a situation, it is a good idea to verify the information independently before taking any action. Our emotions can easily take over and lead us down a slippery slope so do not lose sight of the fact that there are people out there that live and love to find ways to get your money without delivering anything to you in return.

Scammers often prey on people's emotions by taking advantage of their current situations and fears. They might pretend to be sympathetic, understanding, or even offer false promises of support. This can be especially tough when someone is going through a difficult time or seeking help. It is shameful to say, but the more stress you are under, the easier it is for them to catch you with your guard down. I cannot emphasize this enough, but it is essential to be cautious and skeptical, even if someone seems friendly or caring online or through any type of communication.

Remember, protecting yourself from scams is important, and staying informed about common scam tactics can help you avoid falling victim to them. I am sure you have heard the old adage that goes, "It is better to have love and lost than not to have loved at all!" Well, in this instance, it is better not to invest than to invest and lose it all!

Chapter 4: False Promises and Fake Prestige

I cannot explain the growing anticipation of success I felt as the scammer promises of a 'bestseller status' and 'critical acclaim' lured me in more and more. To dream the impossible dream and imagining being able to see my name on the spine of a book overshadowed any skepticism I felt. It sounded like I was in for quite an exciting journey ahead, but in reality, I just did not know what kind of journey I was in for!

"…Country girl done good!"

Imagine me feeling all bubbly with anticipation down to my core. I thought I was on the cusp of something big and life-changing. The scammer, with their silver-tongued promises, whispered the sweet allure of 'best book we have had in many years' and 'we know you have been waiting all your life for this' into my ears and my emotions took over from that point on.

As I envisioned my future I could almost taste and see the success. The thought of my book gracing the bestseller lists and receiving rave reviews from critics and readers alike fueled my imagination and overtook my thoughts. Every word spoken by the scammer seemed like a step closer to living out my dreams. Every conversation was one of reassurances and guarantees that I was making the best decision of my life, and if I could just be patient and hold on a little longer, the life of my family and I would never be the same.

In my mind, scenes played out like a movie – book signings, interviews, and a growing fan base to name a few things. Oh, let us not forget the movie deal I was promised as soon as my book was released….I started to see my name in lights every time I closed my eyes. I felt the satisfaction of accomplishment. With each conversation, my excitement rose and my heart raced at even the prospect of finally achieving the recognition I had always yearned for. But amidst the anticipation, there were flickers of doubt. I could not help but wonder if it was too good to be true. Still, the promises of success kept me hooked, and I found myself entangled in a web of hope and skepticism. Almost like the images we had as children of the devil on one shoulder and Jesus on the other. In this pivotal moment, I stood at the crossroads of my aspirations and lingering uncertainty. I was sure the journey ahead was a rollercoaster full of finances, thrills and emotions. Every word from the scammer (my agent) propelled me further into a thrilling, nerve-wracking, and utterly captivating adventure. I was torn, but not enough to stop the ride!

Scammers often weave intricate tales and exaggerations to maintain control over their victims. They might create elaborate stories about their own success, using fake credentials, photos, and testimonials. These stories can range from portraying themselves as accomplished entrepreneurs to having connections with influential people. By presenting themselves as knowledgeable and trustworthy, scammers manipulate their victims into believing their deceit. Elaborate lies and fabricated success stories are the scammers common tools used to maintain control.

They might share fabricated accounts of their past achievements, such as claiming to have made millions through their business ventures. These tales are designed to create a sense of admiration and aspiration, making victims more likely to trust their advice and invest in their schemes. To maintain control, scammers often employ emotional manipulation, exploiting personal vulnerabilities and desires. For instance, if they know someone is aiming to become a millionaire, they might promise secret investment strategies or exclusive opportunities that require significant upfront payments. These false promises keep victims engaged and invested in the scam.

Scammers also use fake social proof, showing off photo shopped images of luxurious lifestyles, fancy cars, and exotic vacations. They may even invent fictitious success stories from supposed clients who have benefited from their guidance. In reality, these elaborate lies are meant to obscure the scammer's true intentions, which usually involve extracting money or personal information from their victims. It is crucial to stay vigilant, verify credentials, and consult trusted sources before getting involved in any financial or business arrangement.

My strong beliefs in my agent's promises lead me down a path of isolation from my friends and family. I become so convinced that the promises were real that I began neglecting my relationships. I skipped family gatherings, avoided calls, and withdraw from my loved ones because I was told that I needed to be totally focused on the task at hand, and that there are naysayers everywhere, so I had to be careful about whom I talked to about what I was doing.

My isolation was a result of my dedication to pursuing the promises of the scammer, leaving me distant from the very people who cared about me the most. That was the goal…to keep me away from anyone that may have talked some sense into me. The scammers became my family!

Chapter 5: The Dwindling Mirage

When dealing with scammers, it's important to keep an eye out for red flags. Scammers often promise big rewards or benefits but may struggle to provide clear and consistent information. They might change their story or avoid answering specific questions. These are clear indicators that something is amiss. If you are asking about anything financial, and the conversation conveniently switches to something personal or anything besides answering your question, then you have reasons to be skeptical.

If something sounds too good to be true, it probably is. Trust your instincts and double-check any information they provide. Stay cautious and protect yourself from potential scams. If you have any doubts, it is always a good idea to research independently and verify before taking any action. These actions do not discredit who they are but could save you a lot of emotional pain and financial heartache.

It also helps not to get emotionally involved with the people you are going into business with online. We have to be careful overall but it is different doing business in person than when doing business with people that you never get to see unless it is a teleconference. We can gather so much more in regards to how a person deals with us when we have a one-on-one personal relationship with them as oppose to something that is developed over the phone and through emails. In the end though, people let you see what they want you to see and that is where the trap is malicious and vindictive.

I came to the realization that I have been manipulated and deceived; which hit me like a sack of coins going across my face…My life read as a great book would read. I only wish that my story had the happy ending as most books and television shows usually have. I was going through a lot before that email came through about being picked up by a reputable; a 20 year-old publishing company. Even though it took me some time, I began noticing some odd things, like puzzle pieces not fitting together. Slowly, like pieces of a jigsaw, I began seeing the truth: I had been played, manipulated like a puppet. It is like a light bulb moment in a dark room. I remembered conversations, actions, and details that were misleading. The realization hits me like a best-friend betrayal, and it is like a mix of anger, sadness, and shock. My world tilts, and I am left with this sinking feeling that nothing is as it seemed. It is a powerful moment when I understood the reality of my situation; that I had been scammed, and the journey to uncover the full truth begins.

It took me a while to realize that I was the victim of a scam. I did not want to believe it at first but then some things were unavoidable. When reality hits, and you make a decision to face it, it feels like the world has collapsed around your feet. I certainly felt that way. As I am sitting here typing this, those feelings are resurfacing and the memories are like it happened yesterday.

It always amazes me how some people could con, manipulate, and mislead people out of their hard-earned money but the toll is much deeper than finances. I have never fully recovered financially after this occurrence but what I loss in the area of trust left me very skeptical of others as well. I had to learn to trust the people that I knew loved me because I made a decision to trust people that I did not know but they helped me learn a valuable lesson about not checking people out thoroughly. I was always the person that read everything in any contract or agreement, and especially the fine print, but this taught me to get a second opinion about things I do not understand and to also not be lapse in my judgment.

The lies were beginning to not make sense anymore. There is only so much a person can say to you until the inconsistencies begin to mount up. You cannot make sense out of nonsense so the lies that they tried so hard to keep up and the evasiveness was finally recognizable. I had been conned before by different entities and people that would send the phony checks and would try to get you to cash it and you keep some of the money and send them the rest—yes, I fell for that, but this was a different kind of con; one that cut deep!

What really brought the message home was the reality of the amount of money I was out of. You cannot overlook the obvious when it is staring you right in the face or is all gone. My business was doing well at the time and I was attending college at one of the local universities for adult learners. I had money to invest in the dream that I longed for most of my life. I was not guarded when I begin to talk to these people about my finances and that no amount would be too much for me to kick my dream off. I probably sounded like the ideal candidate for the con. They made me feel like I was being given a *bargain* because my talent was so *unique* that they just had to have me so they would be willing to *cut my price* just so I could come on with them. I fell for it.

…and it all came tumbling down.

Chapter 6: The Awakening

It was hard for me to imagine that anything good like this could happen in my life. When you have had a trouble childhood and a hard life, good things seem like things that happened to other people that we watch from afar. At the time the email came, my husband and I were going through a rough patch in our marriage. My 2 youngest children were finished with school so we were empty-nesters, and I felt like something was missing in my life and need a binder to bring it all together.

In my mind, the email came at just the right time. I did not go to school until my kids were out of school. I focused on them and put what I wanted to do on the backburner. I always wanted to go to school, but I began having kids early, and I knew it was my job to see them on their way before I started anything for myself. Now I know some mothers that did go to school and raise their kids, some even worked while doing this, but I chose to work and raise my children. There is no right or wrong way but you have to do what is right for your situation and family setting.

After I read the email, I hastily sent my acceptance to them sending in my contracts and getting the ball rolling. The contract came the next day. I was in amazement that it came so quickly but it was summed up by them stating that they did not want anyone else to snatch me up and wanted me on their roster with their other writers and artist. Everything was happening so fast that I did not have time to think straight. That is where they get you. They hype you up to act without you having time to put things into perspective.

Things moved at lighting speed. It took them 30 days to edit and publish my book. I did not have much say with how things were going because I left many of the decisions to the people I thought were the experts. I went along for the ride and got taken on a journey that I would not wish on anyone. I noticed many hiccups but everything was accounted for and they gave me a level of comfort in knowing that they would take care of all the legalities with their legal department. That made my guard go down even more; not that it was a big guard up anyway. All this was unfamiliar territory and I let my emotions take over instead of doing what I knew to be right and advocating for myself.

I confided in these people my innermost thoughts, talked about my dreams, my unhappiness, my desires; everything that I would discuss with people I knew personally. To be honest, I told them some things that I had only told my best friend that passed away two years ago. They had me on the line like a fish and the bait was winning my trust. If something good happened in a day, I would call my agent and let her know; like we really were good friends or something. I could imagine them laughing at me when we hung up the phone.

The straw that broke the camels back was the day I found out that the company was in bankruptcy and being sued.

The State where the company was based in had also filed a criminal suit against the company, the CEO, and the CFO...Father and son. The father had relinquished rights to the company to the son two years prior but still had interest in the company. The son ran the company into the ground right after he took over. The father was aware of what was going on. If I had done my research, I would have seen all the complaints that the company had against it and the decline that the business experienced after the son took over....IF ONLY I HAD DONE MY RESEARCH!

And so, the investigation begins – bankruptcy, lawsuits, jail terms. What had I missed and what about all the money I had put into my dream. The bills I let go so that I could send money for this or that? The books that I had ordered that I was waiting to receive? Was I still going to New York to meet the other authors at the biggest meet-up the company was going to ever host? The Movie Deal... What was going on and how could I be made whole? So many questions with no answers to make me feel better from the pit that I had drug myself in.

I had to eventually tell my husband about what happened to the money and what was going on in general. I had to face that the money I initially made was probably all the money I was going to make from the book. I had to reconnect with people I had lost contact with because I was told that I only needed the scammers in my life and they were the only people that cared about my writing and my future. I had to make amends with many people.

The hardest struggle of all was the distrust of myself. The knowledge that if I had just slowed down long enough to think instead of falling for the okie-doke, things would not have gotten as bad as they ended up getting. That was a very low time in my life and I thought that the dream was just something in my head that would never happen for me. I thought that good things only happened to other people and I was not in that category. The calling myself *dumb* and *stupid*, among other things, were the hardest connotations to come to terms with. I became my own worst enemy. I blamed myself for letting myself become a statistic!

Chapter 7: Seeking Justice and Redemption

Towards the end, my agent kept trying to get more money out of me. I already had two cases of books on back-order but she wanted me to order two more cases and pay for them. They also wanted me to write my second book and assign it under Bait Publishing, but I would have had to pay all the fees all over again. In all, I paid for a team of editors, a cover artist for the front cover, and a Promo Kit which consists of:

-Promotional copy,

-Promotional Guide for book,

-Marketing Questionnaire,

-Event Publicity Request Form,

-Cover Questionnaire,

-Bookings for Book Signing,

-Book Trailor,

-and a TV Release Form.

The two back-ordered cases never came. I booked my own book signing locally and hired a publicist to help me arrange everything. My agent said that Bait would reimburse me for everything as long as I kept my receipts. The book signing was successful but not because of anything they did; and I never got my money back. I paid for the marketing, the building, food, and all the other accoutrements that come along with a book signing. The cover of the book was cartoonish and in no way represented what the book was about or the seriousness of it.

Later, I found out that the binding was shabby. The books were coming apart at the seams. That was because they did not pay the employees at the publishing company that did that job, so they had to get it done overseas. That is why it took so long for the books to come back. Initially, they offered me cases of 50, 100, and 200. I ordered a case of 200, which is what I sold personally and at the book signing, then followed that up with (2) 200 cases. I was selling more myself then they were. Nothing they had me pay for was done because ultimately, I discovered that the editing was not done as well. Talking about adding insult to injury.

"A Cartoonish book cover (that was not even the standard book size), pages falling out of the books, and a raw book with no edits!"

Everything hit the fan when another author reached out to me to see if I had heard that Bait was under investigation and had filed for bankruptcy…I had heard no such thing but then I began researching. My eyes became fully open at this point. I googled them and everything began showing up; EVERYTHING!

I tried calling and I could not get anyone. I emailed and nothing was returned. I then called every number that I had for anyone that I ever spoke with at Bait and no one was reachable. In my heart, I knew that my agent was up to her neck in whatever was going on, but I wanted to believe she was innocent in all of this, so I called the number she gave me that was supposed to be her personal number. It was disconnected. At this point, the doors were locked and the company was shut down.

My wounds were deep and the flood of emotions that ran through me were so unbalanced until I did not know if I was coming or going at times. I would have periods of crying, I would shut down, I would be snappy…I was all over the place emotionally. I could not believe that this could happen to me and that I probably would never recover financially.

I found out that the Attorney General of the State in which Bait was located took up a case against them and wanted anyone that thought they may have been scammed by Bait to reach out to them. The social media group I was in shared a wealth of information and I discovered the link to send my information. I had to prove that I was an author signed with Bait by faxing my contract, all receipts I received from them, and proof of everything I paid for with the company. I am one of those people that keeps everything, so I was able to provide proof of everything they were asking for. When I sat at my kitchen table, and added everything up, that is when the tears really began to flow.

I also had to answer a 15-page inquiry from the courts. One of the details I had to explain is what made me ultimately sign a contract with the company. In the earlier chapters, I stated that I was going to reveal how I let my guard down and Bait Publishing was able to rob me. I know the terminology sounds extreme but that is what they did. They robbed me of my money, my dignity, my trust in others and myself. How did this happen? How were they able to make me feel so comfortable until I let all my guard down? Well, during the earlier conversations, I was a little hesitant in the beginning, but I was soon put at eased when in one of the conversations between myself and my agent, I shared about my mother passing as a victim of domestic violence when I was three years old and of the dreams I was having that ended up being abuse that happened to me as a child and I was trying to get myself together to write about it in my next book. The agent got quiet then asked me could she share something with me off the record. Now she said off the record, but all conversations were recorded, and the recording did not stop for this conversation…Anyway, she ended up telling me that she lost her mother when she was a mere baby and she too was molested as a child and had a horrible childhood. We both broke down and cried that day. I resolved at that time that I could trust this lady and the company because she said that she shared her background with the company; and they embraced her and eased her. She said that Bait Publishing were her family and she would trust them with her life. This made me want to make them my family and to have that sense of belonging to something that was bigger than I.

Well, the lawsuit ended up being bigger than I. Not trying to make light of it, but after it all is said and done, that is what kept me going; a sense of humor, but it took a long time to get to that point. After all the formalities were finished, and everything turned in, we had to wait. The waiting period was the worst experience ever. Seemed like time moved in slow motion. It lingered for over two years; from early 2016-February 2018. During that time, they gave Bait the opportunity to give us our Rights back to our books. You are reading this correctly…they had the rights to our books. I filled out a request form and emailed it to the email address they had listed. Even though they were not operational, they had some employees to answer email for a short period of time. What we got back was a payment request for $250, the requests were from $50-$500, and then they said they would sell us our rights to our property. Do you all think I paid that? Some people did but I did not. I was not going to give them one more brown cent. I had already given them my dignity and had nothing else to give.

I found out that legally they could not do that because they did not honor their end of the contract, so everything was null and void. I was elated to hear this. They tried to stick it to us one last time, but they ended up with two additional counts added to their long list of charges because they accepted the payments from the victims that did pay the hostage amount. This experience truly was a nightmare.

When it was all done, they had to pay us restitution, but it was pennies on the dollar. Mine was set for ten years. I get $3.13 four times a year. I do not think that is really pennies on my dollar. I was sad and upset about it for a long time but then it turned to anger. I wanted to make sure that nothing like this happened to anyone again and to let other new authors know that they had to protect themselves by doing their due diligence no matter how great something sounded. It is not going to hurt to check things out but it can do major damage if you do not.

The Social Media group helped us to have a proactive approach in warning fellow authors and collaborating with others who have been scammed. We embodied the importance of creating a supportive community where people could share their experiences and learn from each other's challenges. By doing this, we not only helped others avoid potential pitfalls but also fostering a sense of solidarity among authors. Sharing stories, strategies, and resources went a long way in safeguarding the creative and entrepreneurial efforts of everyone involved.

My family and friends were also a great support during this time. Though I never told anyone the exact amount, they knew it was a lot of money and tried their best to keep my spirits lifted. Honestly, I did not know if I wanted my spirits lifted. I wanted to feel in the dumps because I was dumped on, but they would not let me have my pity-party, and a day did not go by where I did not get a phone call, text, or a visitor checking on me. That was very important to me and key in me being able to bounce back from this terrible ordeal.

I always loved helping other people, but this gave me a sense of urgency to really step out and be vocal about the potential risk to new authors, and to share what happened to me, so that their journey would not turn into trauma. Healing and building back my self-confidence were a journey and I embraced it while staying connected to my faith and other interests.

Chapter 8: Rebuilding the Narrative

I needed to explore my journey of self-discovery and introspection to delve deep to figure out what was lacking in me to allow myself to be lured into something like this scam. What was missing in my life that had me to succumb to this juncture of embarrassment and humiliation. Would I be able to narrow it down was the question that I desperately needed to answer.

Through this journey, I reflected a lot on many things. I thought about my life as far back as I could remember and all I could think of was the pain I endured from the people that were closest to me. The more I thought about it, the more sense it made. When someone gets conned, the criminal has to find something to connect with so that they can make that person feel like they are the missing piece to make their life whole. For me, that moment happened when the agent connected with the emotions I felt of losing my mother at a young age and being molested. Those were factors that impacted my whole life and Bait was able to use one person to lure me into the trap by bringing the thing that I longed for all my life into one place…This was huge for me. I never knew that not having my mother in my life impacted me so deeply. I did not realize that the events of my past still had me bound. Discovering these things meant that I could properly heal and not be bound anymore.

I then began to meditate and finding other things I enjoyed doing. I looked up long lost friends and relatives that I had lost track of and engaged in deep conversations. I had to rebuild relationship that I tore down when I had put all my trust in Bait. Those moments helped me uncover layers of my personality and gain insights into my past and present. I realized both were connected and I needed to fully tap into my past so that I could move into my present; without the baggage moving with me!

As I evolved, I learned to accept my flaws and embrace my strengths. Even though this journey involved some twists and turns, much like life itself, it taught me to adapt and grow. I grew strong enough to begin sharing my insights with others through writing and speaking. Overall, it was a process of becoming more self-aware of my beauty, intelligence, abilities, and vulnerabilities. My journey was unique, but it was all about discovering who I was at the core and how I fit into this space of being.

It was a difficult experience going through with the scam. Overcoming emotional scars can be challenging, but through my life, I always had a resilient spirit, and that is what it took to get through this. I wanted to reclaim my passion for writing because I did not want to write anything after what I had went through. I wanted to get as far away from a laptop, tablet, or a notebook as was humanly possible, but I could not let go of what was so deeply a part of me since I was a little girl. I began slowly by jotting down my thoughts, feelings, and even my experiences dealing with the scam. This helped me process my emotions and gradually get back into the groove of writing. I surrounded myself with positive influences and the outdoors that I loved. I always had a connection with water, and I would go to one of our local parks often to look at the ducks and just gaze into the water. I took things one step at a time and give myself the space I needed to heal. All of this came along after I forgave myself for the pitfall I ended up sliding into!

Chapter 9: Lessons Learned

This is going to sound really crazy, but in some ways, I am thankful that this happened to me. It was not good on my bank account and NO, it did not feel good when I was going through it. The rebuilding process was difficult, but I have so many take-a-ways from this adventure until it was enough to put into this book. I am going to break them down step by step:

Reflect and Reevaluate: I took a moment to reflect on my writing journey. What worked well and what did not. Could I do what I paid people to do that they did not do at all? Could I edit my own book? Could I self-publish? Could I market it myself or find someone at a reasonable cost to do it. Could I do my own book signing? Well, I did do my own book signing so of course I could do it again. This self-assessment helped me understand my strengths and areas that I needed to improve. I realized that fear was holding me back from stepping out and doing the work to become that author I always wanted to be but we will not know what we can do unless we try. We also cannot be afraid of failure. Failure hurts sometimes but it lets us know what direction to take if something did not work. Chart your failures and move on to success!!!

Set Clear Goals: I had to define what I wanted to achieve with my writing career. I did want to write more books, I wanted to learn how to do the things that lazily I paid for. I also wanted to help others with their conception, layout, editing, and show them how to self-publish their book once I learned how to do it. I also wanted to learn all that I could about this journey. Bait did get my book to best seller. The first royalty check I received was for $420. I thought that check would be the first of many but sadly, that was the only check I received. It sold great on major book platform and on Bait's website, but I received none of what was due to me after that first check. I wanted to set myself up in a way where I had control of what I sold from my book. I wanted to be able to keep up with my stats. I basically wanted control of my body of work because the hostage amount that Bait tried to get from me taught me a valuable lesson about having control of your intellectual property. I had a clear image of what I wanted to do and how I wanted to do it. It would take time and research.

Create a Plan: My research helped me to create an outline for a practical plan of action. I broke down my larger goals into smaller, achievable ones. For example, since I already knew I wanted to write more books, I set milestones for research, writing, and editing. I also did not want to go too far with the books I had in my head until I had a clear path to what I was going to do with the book I already had published. I decided that, how my mind works, that I could write a book and get started on the next book before I finished one. I would lay out my outline and have it ready for whenever I was ready to begin the next book.

Allocate Time Wisely: As an Ordained Minister, entrepreneur, President and Founder of a nonprofit, social advocate, and all the other various interests I had (and still have), time management was crucial. Writing sets your creative juices flowing but you also must have a clear mind for those juices to even blend. I decided I would write when my schedule permitted and when I could focus totally on my craft. It is nothing to be able to belt out chapters at a time, but I wanted to be able to have substance in my book, and not feel rushed in writing it. The best books have one or two mistakes, but if you take the time to do it right the first time, when you go back over it, you will not have too much to correct. Take your time and set yourself up for success. That is what I wanted to do. I set aside dedicated time slots for writing, my business, and my many other activities. Consistency and determination are key.

Expand Your Network: I was not always a social person, but now being an outgoing person, I learned to leverage my socializing skills to connect with fellow writers locally and in other cities. I approached it the same way I did my business except with a different niche. I found people that was willing to show me the things I needed to learn. Some was for free and some at a small cost, but these were people I knew and trusted, so I knew I would get the knowledge I was paying for. Networking opened doors to collaborations and learning opportunities that I embraced. It also opened the door for speaking engagements since my book was about an occurrence in my life that I was very passionate about. I was nervous about it at first, but I believed in myself enough to know that I could do it and be successful at it.

Embrace Learning: I mentioned above about being open to learning everything there was to learn about my craft. It is more to being an author than just writing. Sure, I loved writing, but not knowing what I was supposed to look for and be educated about on is what got me in this situation in the first place, so I studied various materials. I also kept up with industry trends, writing techniques, and writing strategies. Continuous learning keeps my content fresh and engaging even until this day. What I learned has took me a long way in my healing. It made me confident that I could spot ill-will well in advance before I got caught up in a losing situation. Money is hard to come by. Things are hard for everyone, and I did not want to be put in that kind of financial situation again from a lackadaisical decision, so I learned with intent and purpose.

Practice Patience: Rebuilding takes time, so I did not rush the process. I am a very laid-back person in general so that helped me not to rush and to go steady with applying what I was learning. I did not let my situation determine my timeline. I could have rushed, but then that would have turned up in my work, so I remained patient and focused as I worked toward my goals.

Seek Guidance: I was not too proud to ask for help in the areas that I felt needed personal learning instead of virtual or googling. This is where networking really helped me get in touch with the people that I knew already were doing what I dreamed of doing. I connected with mentors and peers who have successfully built writing careers. Their insights provided valuable guidance and encouragement for me after the ordeal I was coming out of.

Adapt and Pivot: I had to be open to adjusting my approach based on feedback and results. I had to learn not to be so consumed with a concept that I am not able to abort if it is not working. If I discovered that certain strategies were not yielding the desired outcomes, I did not hesitate to pivot. Being too focused and self-centered on one of our ideas can be damaging. If you spend too much time on something that is not working, then you miss out on the time that could have been spent on a viable concept. Time is precious and valuable; use it wisely!

Stay Positive: My rebuilding process was very challenging. It was difficult to try and be positive while going through the worst ordeal of my life. The two years we went through the court proceedings, I did not write at all. I did not want to even think about writing. I was broken and my life was in limbo. That would have shown in anything I wrote. My Faith carried me through though. I knew that even though I felt defeated, and I had no money in my account, I could celebrate small victories, and remember that setbacks are part of the journey. Celebrating the small victories led to building up my confidence and helped me to become positive about rebuilding my writing career. I had to know that I could do it and this tragedy did not define who I was but was a part of my evolving story, which is life.

Incorporate Balance: While chasing my goals, I had to remember to spend quality time with my family and friends. I could remember a time when my nonprofit always had something on the calendar for Saturdays, plus I would have my business and meetings during the week. One time during an argument, my husband told me to look at the calendar. I did not know what he was referring to. He said, "Where do I fit in Tonia?" That made me realize that I had to do better with my time. I had to make sure that my family did not feel left out. We can have a busy schedule, but we must not only make sure that we are setting priorities for the things we do and to not schedule our family but let them know they matter by having that time available. I could not get too caught up on one thing, and then must make up in the lacking area once something got behind, so balance contributed to my overall well-being and creativity.

Celebrate Progress: It is not only important to celebrate successes but to celebrate any progress that you make in your comeback journey. We must acknowledge our achievements along the way. Whether it is completing a chapter, reaching a milestone in life, or getting closer to our goals; celebrate each step forward.

Personally, every step of the court process was healing for me, and I celebrated. Every inditement, every sentence that was handed down, even the mere fraction on the dollar that was awarded to us was reason to celebrate the progress that was being made through the case and it helped me to be able to smile again. It would not help me get the thousands I lost but it would help me build back something that money cannot buy; belief in myself.

I have practical advice for new authors to avoid falling victim to similar scams: It is important to share insights on the lessons that are learned through positive and negative experiences. I learned both from this scam experience and I advise new authors to steer clear of such situations. I learned some crucial lessons from my ordeal.

First, I had to realize that not everyone in the publishing or business world has good intentions. It is essential to be cautious and do thorough research before committing to any deals.

Second, I discovered the importance of seeking advice from a supportive community. Having a network of experienced peers can provide valuable insights and warnings about potential scams.

Lastly, the experience taught me to always trust my instincts. If something feels off or too good to be true, it probably is.

For new authors, avoiding scams requires a mix of common sense and diligence. Do not just jump in without finding out what is required to pursue your new passion. Surround yourself with a community of fellow authors or mentors who can guide you through the industry. These connections can help you spot red flags, and they can also share their experiences.

Research is your best friend when done correctly and not hurried. Investigate any publishing offers thoroughly, look for reviews, testimonials, and any negative experiences from other authors. Do not rush into any decision. Take your time to review contracts, understand terms, and ask many questions. If they feel uncomfortable by you asking questions or try to avoid giving you a straight answer while just wanting you to sign and pay up, then that is not the publishing house for you.

Sidebar: In any venture you are trying to get into, this is a BIG RED STOP SIGN!!!

Be careful with any upfront fees or promises of instant success. Legitimate publishers earn money when your book sells, not by asking you for money upfront. This action is a clear warning to stay clear. I am not saying that all offers like this are scams, but a large majority are. Make sure you are comfortable with the entire process, and have done your proper research, before committing to any terms or turning over any funds.

I cannot emphasize enough the importance of community, research, and due diligence. Community, research, and due diligence are like your trusty trio in avoiding scams. Building relationships with other authors and professionals creates a safety net of advice and warnings. Research arms you with knowledge about the industry, publisher backgrounds, and potential warning signs. Due diligence is all about taking the time to investigate, ask questions, and consult with others before making decisions. Remember, it is better to be safe than sorry.

Always stay true to your goals, keep pursuing your passions, and use wisdom before being hesitant!

A combination of caution, wisdom, determination, and faith guided me through my rebuilding process. I stayed true to my passions and stayed the course; and success followed.

Conclusion: The Power of Resilience

This journey taught me that I am not just a vulnerable dreamer, but I am a resilient survivor. Resilience is like a superpower that helps us bounce back when life throws us curveballs like setbacks and betrayals; and this was a bitter betrayal on the worst level. It is all about being tough in a gentle way, like a tree that bends but does not break in a storm. When we face tough times, or when someone we trust lets us down, resilience helps us stay strong and find our footing again.

Think of it as a mix of mental toughness and emotional flexibility. Resilience does not mean ignoring the pain; it means acknowledging it and finding ways to heal and move forward. I could not ignore how I felt but I did not let it define who I was. Most of us probably have experienced setbacks and disappointments because everyone goes through them. The level of the setback determines the depth of the hurt. Resilience helps us learn from these experiences, adapt, and even grow stronger instead of sinking into a deep depression.

It is like our muscles that gets stronger with exercise. When we face challenges head-on, we build up our resilience muscles. And having that resilience can be a game-changer in reaching our goals and desired. Setbacks and betrayals might slow us down for a moment, but with resilience, we will keep moving forward and achieving those amazing things we are aiming for.

Resilience is that inner strength we all have – it is about bouncing back when life throws us disappointments. When setbacks and betrayals hit, they can really shake us up. Being resilient means not letting those punches keep us down for long.

Think of it like a basketball game. Sometimes, your team falls behind or the opponent makes an unexpected move. It is frustrating, but you do not just give up, right? You keep pushing, strategizing, and adapting. Resilience is that same spirit applied to life. We must keep pushing forward and only look back to learn the lesson not to delve into sadness and self-pity.

Facing setbacks teaches us valuable lessons. It can be compared to training for a marathon. We do not start out being able to run 26.2 miles, but with training and resilience, we build up to it. Betrayals, on the other hand, can feel like getting tackled from behind. They hurt and break trust, but being resilient helps us heal and move forward.

Remember, even the strongest trees sway during a storm, but they do not break. Resilience is our ability to sway with life's challenges and not break under pressure. And over time, as we practice resilience, we become more flexible and better equipped to handle whatever comes our way.

So, when setbacks and betrayals come knocking, remember the basketball game, the marathon, and the swaying tree. Stay strong, learn from the experiences, and keep moving forward. You know and believe that you got this!

I want this book to leave you with a sense of hope, empowerment and to encourage you to pursue your dreams while staying vigilant. Our dreams are the fuel that drives us forward. They are like stars guiding us through the night. It is crucial to believe in yourself and your potential. Do not let anyone deter you from the power that you have within. Life might throw challenges your way, but each obstacle is an opportunity in disguise. Do not see the glass half empty but half full. Stay focused on your goals, and do not be afraid to adapt and learn from setbacks.

Surround yourself with positivity, both in people and in your mindset. Just like a garden needs nurturing, your dreams require constant effort and care. Embrace your journey, step by step, and do not hesitate to seek inspiration from others who have walked similar paths. Remember, you are not alone on this journey. Your determination and resilience will light up the path to your dreams. So keep pushing forward, and never underestimate the power of your own potential!

Sidebar...DO NOT DEPEND FULLY ON SOCIAL MEDIA. Social media can be an amazing tool to market your book and advertise BUT most of the people on your social media are people that you know. Try to have a budget to utilize other outlets for a new audience. Our families want to support us, but we cannot bombard them and make them feel obligated to. Even for your own growth, search out other outlets to get your book out there without only relying on social media, friends, and family.

Epilogue: A New Chapter

These days, I am doing quite well and making steady progress. I am a successful entrepreneur, I have published 5 books-more on that in a minute, I have a podcast called, A Womans Soul: Restored, and I am pursuing my passions of being a playwright. I also edit books professionally now and I help others on their journey to self-publishing. The first time you try to publish a book, it can be a scary process, but I coach potential authors every step of the way. The only skill I have not mastered is marketing. Whew, that is a story within itself. If I can master that, it would be amazing but kudos to those that have it under their belt.

I still love to read, meditate, and spend time outdoors; embracing my creative side. I am also focused on my newest goal of getting a new car this year and working towards becoming a multi-millionaire. Your read right. I aim big these days. My dedication to helping others and leading my family to Christ is a reoccurring aspiration that

I strive to accomplish daily. I have a commitment to my personal growth and sharing my wisdom.

I have two grandchildren now. My granddaughter who was born on July 20, 2018 by my daughter and my grandson who was born November 30, 2018 by my youngest son. Yep, for 8 months, they are the same age. They are a handful, but they are my joy, and my sense of being. They ground me to see the potential for the next generation. I see my genes in them and want to teach them everything I humanly can.

The organization is still doing well. We lost some footing during Covid, just as the world came to a standstill, we did as well. The road has not been easy to recover from but just like anything else, we have had to have a drive and determination to get back to where we were or better.

Business fluctuates but that is the life of an entrepreneur. The highs are very high, oh but those lows…that is where planning and saving goes a long way.

Overall, my journey is marked by achievements and a strong desire to make a positive impact on the world.

Now about those books…

I got my full rights back for my original book and ended up doing a second edition on July 25, 2018. I was able to do my edits myself, change the cover, and give the book an overhaul by adding content that was not in the original and extending the name from "Issues of the Male Heart" to "Issues of the Male Heart; When His Issues Become Your Issues!". I was very thankful that I did not give up on my project and I was able to have complete control over my work.

A Window Without A View was published on October 12, 2018. No, this is not a mistake. I was writing this book while editing the other and self-published both a few months apart. In the beginning, this book did not even sell 50 copies, but one of those people reached out to me because they had a syndicated network and introduced me to the world of podcasting. My podcast was on their platform and the book and podcast took off.

The 13 Principles of Womanship: The Christian Woman Guide to Effective Leadership was published on October 21, 2018. All proceeds from this book goes to benefit Sisters Helping Sisters Social Org. for Women, Inc.

The Soul of Joy was published on April 23, 2020 and sold as a best seller in it's own right. I was so proud of this book because Bait helped my first book to get to best seller status but kept my royalties. This book was my baby, and I was happy to finally be able to live my dream of being an author. I wrote this book at a very low time in my life with my husband right on the cusp of Covid 19.

When the Storm Came, God Helped Us to STAND! was published April 13, 2022 on my 20th Anniversary being married to my husband. This book was our story and the trials that plagued our marriage…But God is all I can say.

I have found 'life after Bait' and I am able to do the thing that I have loved since childhood. Some days I cry because of the joy I feel in my soul. When you have had a hard life, the good things that happen can seem like a dream that eventually you are going to wake up from. Life is full of inconsistencies, but life is also a beautiful instrument that plays a song made specifically just for us individually.

Writing, just like life, is a journey filled with twists and turns. As you venture into the realm of becoming an author, remember that your uniqueness is your greatest asset. Your experiences, perspectives, and ideas are what will make your voice stand out in a crowded world of words.

There will be moments when self-doubt creeps in, and challenges might seem insurmountable. But here is the thing: adversity is a powerful teacher. Embrace it, learn from it, and let it fuel your growth. Every rejection and every setback are a stepping-stone toward honing your craft.

Stay true to yourself. Your authenticity is what will resonate with readers. Pour your heart into your words, and do not be afraid to tackle subjects that matter to you, even if they are tough. Remember, vulnerability can be a bridge that connects your words with the hearts of your readers.

The path of an author requires patience and perseverance. It is not about immediate success, but the impact you make over time. Keep writing, keep refining, keep pushing yourself to evolve. Surround yourself with fellow writers who understand the journey and draw inspiration from your love of personal growth and your connection to self-discovery.

Believe in your ability to overcome challenges. Depending on what type of life you have lived, life had already taught you how to overcome adversity. This is key, because if I did not know how to overcome this scam, I would not have been able to move on and achieve success in the thing that almost cost me everything. The ability to see past your circumstances is an anchor to help you remember that trials come, and sometimes they come fast and hard, but just like the last trial you overcame, you will overcome the current one too. Think about it…that thing that you thought was the end really was not the end because you are still here, and as long as you are still here, there are opportunities to do great and be great.

Keep the faith, keep writing, and keep touching lives with your words. Your story matters, and through your dedication and determination, you will inspire others to chase their dreams too. Your perseverance will be a beacon of hope for aspiring authors who dare to dream and work hard to make those dreams come true. Each tribulation is a lesson in life to help you get to the next level.

Do not give up; keep striving and pushing ahead!!!

Issues Of The
Heart Male
When His Issues
ecome Your Issues.
Issues
of the
Heart
Male

Made in the USA
Columbia, SC
15 February 2025